DEEP-SEA
FISHING

By William David Thomas

Reading Consultant: Susan Nations, M.Ed.,
author/literacy coach/consultant in literacy development

Gareth Stevens
Publishing

Please visit our web site at **www.garethstevens.com**.
For a free catalog describing Gareth Stevens Publishing's list of high-quality books, call 1-800-542-2595 (USA) or 1-800-387-3178 (Canada).
Gareth Stevens Publishing's fax: 1-877-542-2596

Library of Congress Cataloging-in-Publication Data

Thomas, William David.
    Deep-sea fishing / William David Thomas.
        p. cm.—(Cool careers. Adventure careers)
    Includes bibliographical references and index.
        ISBN-10: 0-8368-8881-2   ISBN-13: 978-0-8368-8881-2 (lib. bdg.)
        ISBN-10: 0-8368-8888-X   ISBN-13: 978-0-8368-8888-1 (softcover)
    1. Big game fishing—Juvenile literature.   2. Fisheries—Vocational guidance—Juvenile literature.   I. Title.
    SH457.5.T46   2007
    634.9'618023—dc22   2007027664

This edition first published in 2008 by
Gareth Stevens Publishing
A Weekly Reader® Company
1 Reader's Digest Road
Pleasantville, NY 10570-7000 USA

Senior Managing Editor: Lisa M. Guidone
Managing Editor: Valerie J. Weber
Creative Director: Lisa Donovan
Designer: Paula Jo Smith
Cover Photo Researcher: Kimberly Babbitt
Interior Photo Researcher: Susan Anderson

Picture credits: Cover, title page © 2007 Steven Kazlowski/AlaskaStock.com; pp. 4–5 © John Hyde/Alaska Stock; p. 6 Map Resources; p. 9 © Natalie Forbes/Corbis; p. 10 © Ralph A. Clevenger/Corbis; p. 11 © Charles E. Rotkin/Corbis; pp. 12–13 © 2007 Chris Arend/Alaska Stock; pp. 14–15 © Nik Wheeler/Corbis; p. 17 Everett Collection; p. 19 © Richard Bickel/Corbis; p. 20 Karen Kasmauski/Corbis; p. 21 Richard Cummins/Corbis; p. 23 Joe Raedle/Getty Images; pp. 25, 27 © Galen Rowell/Corbis; p. 29 © Dave Bartruff/Corbis

Printed in the United States of America

CPSIA Compliance Information: For further information contact Gareth Stevens, New York, New York at 1-800-542-2595

CONTENTS

Words in the glossary appear in **bold** type the first time they are used in the text.

CHAPTER 1
ADVENTURE ON THE SEA

Think about the gym in your school. Imagine you are standing on the floor, looking up at the ceiling. Now think about a wave of water as high as that ceiling. It is coming toward you. Imagine you're on the deck of a boat that is bouncing up and down and rolling from side to side. And that huge wave is coming closer.

Deep-sea fishermen often face that kind of danger. High waves and strong winds are part of their work. So are thick fog and bitter cold. Fishermen may work among whales or icebergs. They may have to steer their small boats among huge ships.

Up from the sea! Hundreds of pounds of salmon fill the net of this fishing boat off the coast of Alaska.

How dangerous is it? More than one-third of deep-sea fishermen are injured every year. They are twenty times more likely to die on the job than workers in any other business.

These people risk their lives to bring fish, oysters, shrimp, and lobsters to our grocery stores. In spite of the danger, most of these men and women love their work. They wouldn't want to do anything else.

Deep-Sea Fishing Grounds

The areas shown in red are
fishing grounds described in this book.

Chukchi Sea
Whaling Grounds

ALASKA

Alaskan Salmon
Fishing Grounds

Canada

PACIFIC
OCEAN

United States

Grand Banks Cod
Fishing Grounds

ATLANTIC
OCEAN

Mexico

Gulf Coast Shrimp
Fishing Grounds

Learning the Job

How do you become a deep-sea fisherman? For
people who live near the ocean, it's a natural job.
For many of them, fishing is a family business.

For others, it's only part-time work. There are no schools that teach deep-sea fishing. It has to be learned "on the job," and there is a lot to learn.

All fishermen have to know about nets, lines, hooks, and small boats. They must be mechanics, too. Fishermen often have to fix engines and other gear. And they must know how to "read the water." To do so, they look at the changing color of the sea, the shape of waves, and where the waves come from. These changes may warn fishermen of danger or tell them where to find fish.

Modern fishing boats carry a lot of electronic gear. All of them have radios, and many have **sonar.** Some have computers as well. The captain and crew must know how to use all this equipment. Boat captains must know **navigation.** And, of course, someone on a fishing boat has to be the cook.

Love of the Sea

Fishermen work in all of the oceans around the United States. The boats and equipment they use are different. So are the fish they catch.

But in one way, these men and women are all alike. All of them love the adventure of deep-sea fishing.

CHAPTER 2
THE SALMON FISHERMEN OF ALASKA

I t is spring in the northern Pacific Ocean. Beneath the waves, something strange is happening. Big fish called salmon are forming into groups. These groups — sometimes thousands of fish — are swimming together. The salmon are all swimming toward the same place — Alaska. A big welcome awaits them. Hungry sharks and seals wait for the salmon to come. Bears look for them along rivers and streams. Eagles watch for salmon from the sky. People welcome their return, too. Every spring, Alaskan fishermen wait for the salmon to "run."

Controlling the Run

These big fish are worth a lot of money. Salmon caught in Alaska each year are worth nearly $250 million. Strict limits are set on fishing, however. The limits tell fishermen when — and for how long — they can fish. If too many fish are caught, too few will **reproduce.** The population will drop quickly. These limits make sure there will always salmon to catch.

Wildlife officers watch for the salmon. When the time is right, they say fishing can begin. The times

Hungry brown bears in Alaska wait for salmon leaping up a waterfall.

when people can fish are called "openings." They are usually short. An opening may last only one or two days. The number of openings is different each year, depending on how many fish are running. The salmon fishermen wait and listen. When an opening is announced, they go out to sea.

Gillnetters

During an opening, salmon fishermen work twenty-four hours a day. That's where the danger begins. It's easy to make a mistake when you are very tired. And there isn't much help. Fishing crews are small. Most boats have only three or four people. Some salmon fishermen go out alone.

Most Alaskan salmon fishermen are **gillnetters.** This means they use large nets to catch the fish. The nets have floats along the top edge. Boats pull the nets just below the water's surface. The openings in the net are large enough for smaller fish to get out, but big salmon can't. They are "gilled."

A Great Mystery

Salmon swim up streams to lay their eggs. After the eggs hatch, the tiny fish stay in their home stream for many months. As they grow, they begin to swim downstream toward the ocean. When they reach the Pacific Ocean, they swim thousands of miles away. After several years, the same fish will return to the same stream where they were hatched. Scientists know that this happens. They just don't know how or why. It is one of the great mysteries of nature.

Gillnetter boats have large nets to catch a lot of salmon.

Gillnet boats have a large drum at the **bow** or the **stern.** The boat's engine powers the drum, which lets out or pulls in the net. This can be a dangerous time. Fingers or hands caught against the drum can be crushed. Fishermen caught in the nets may be pulled overboard.

More Danger

Sharks often follow the boats. A net full of salmon is like a lunch box for them. Sharks sometimes tear open the nets. If they get caught inside, they end up on the deck of the boat when the net is pulled in. The thrashing tail of an angry shark can slam crew members against railings and masts. Its snapping jaws can leave them bleeding from deep wounds.

One of the greatest dangers is falling into the water. Even in summer, the water near Alaska is very cold. Being in the water for just a short time can cause **hypothermia.** People become too cold to swim, and they drown.

The ocean is always dangerous. High waves and strong winds are common during fishing season. Gillnet boats can be pushed into rocks, and waves can easily turn them over. Every year, more than thirty fishing boats sink. Every year, more than twenty fishermen die. But every year, the fishermen of Alaska go to sea when the salmon run.

Big Leapers

The scientific name for salmon is *Salmonidae,* which means "leaper." When salmon "run," they swim up rivers and streams. They often come to **rapids** or waterfalls. Salmon leap over them, sometimes jumping as high as 10 feet (3 meters). Dams have blocked some rivers. In those places, "ladders" have been built for the salmon. These small pools are built-in steps. Salmon leap from one pool to the next to get past the dam.

13

CHAPTER 3
THE GRAND BANKERS

More than five hundred years ago, an English sea captain named John Cabot sailed near Canada. He came to a place where the sea was shallow. There, Cabot saw more fish than he had ever seen before. They were cod. There were so many, Cabot said he could have walked on them. The captain's "fish walk" became known as the Grand Banks.

From Sail to Steam

Small sailing ships began coming to the Banks carrying little rowboats called **dories.** One or two men worked in each dory, using hand-held lines with big hooks to catch cod. The fish were cut up, salted, and stored in the ship. Ships would stay on the Banks until their **holds** were full of cod.

A fisherman in Newfoundland, Canada prepares his catch for market.

Deep-sea fishing in small ships and dories was very dangerous. Hooks caught hands and arms as easily as they caught fish. The Banks are very foggy, and dories often got lost. Some were never seen again. Every year, ships sank in storms.

In the early 1900s, steam-powered ships began fishing the Banks. They used huge nets to catch fish. This was dangerous, too. Sometimes men got caught in nets and were pulled overboard. And the weather was still a danger. The new ships were bigger and stronger, but they were no match for the storms on the Grand Banks.

By the 1960s, cod and other fish were harder to find. Too many had been caught. Ships from many countries still came to the Banks to fish. Each country claimed part of the Banks. They said boats from other countries could not fish there. This led to new dangers.

Cod Wars and Sword Boats

Fishermen began to fight each other. Boat crews cut the nets of other boats. Boats rammed into other boats to chase them from the fishing grounds. During the 1970s, ships from Great Britain and Iceland fired guns at each other. Newspapers called it the "Cod Wars."

Today, the cod are nearly gone. Some countries have **banned** cod fishing on the Banks. Many fishermen have quit. Those who remain look for other kinds of fish.

Swordfish are caught on the Banks now. "Sword boats" drop long lines into the sea. The lines have hundreds of big hooks, baited with chunks of fish. Swordfish can weigh up to 1,000 pounds (455 kilograms). They have been known to attack small boats and are very dangerous to bring on board a ship. Their long, sharp bills can easily cut fishermen.

In October 1991, a huge storm struck the Grand Banks. Author Sebastian Junger wrote about a sword boat that was lost in the storm. His book, *The Perfect Storm*, became a hit movie in 2000.

Fishing the Grand Banks is still a dangerous job. The men and women doing it hope the cod will come back. They hope to keep fishing for many more years.

Huge waves roll in this scene from the film *The Perfect Storm*. The *Andrea Gail* was a real swordfish boat that sank near the Grand Banks in a 1991 storm.

Streams in the Ocean

The Gulf Stream is a warm **current** in the ocean. It flows northward along the east coast of the United States, then bends out into the Atlantic Ocean. There, it meets a band of cold water flowing south, called the Labrador Current. These two streams meet in the Grand Banks. Their movement lifts **nutrients** from the ocean floor. These nutrients feed small sea creatures. In turn, these creatures become food for fish. This combination of warm and cold water creates the perfect spot for fish to live and grow.

CHAPTER 4

THE GULF COAST SHRIMPERS

The sun is rising on the Gulf of Mexico. Under the sea, millions of shrimp are digging holes in the sand and mud. They will hide there during the day. On shore, Gulf Coast shrimpers are getting ready for work. They hope to find the shrimp and catch them. More than

The Dead Zone

Rivers carry pollution into the Gulf of Mexico. It comes from fertilizers washed off farms and from chemicals dumped by factories. It all flows into the Gulf. The polluted part of the Gulf is called the Dead Zone. The pollution helps algae grow. The algae take oxygen from the water. All animals need oxygen to live. Where algae grow, nothing else can live. The Dead Zone gets bigger every year. Scientists, fishermen, and others are trying to stop the pollution so shrimp, fish, and other sea creatures can live there once again.

The shrimp boat *Miss Wanda* anchors in the Gulf of Mexico.

200 million pounds (91 million kg) of shrimp are caught along the Gulf Coast each year. The catch is worth over $400 million.

Beam Trawling

Shrimp boats are called **trawlers.** They carry nets that are 20 to 30 feet (6 to 9 m) long. Boats have one or two nets on each side. At the front of each net is a long, heavy bar called a beam, which makes the front end of the net sink. The boat pulls it along the bottom

of the sea. The beam kicks up the sand and mud —
and the hidden shrimp. They are swept into the net.

Every two hours or so, the nets are hauled up.
Electric motors help pull in the heavy nets and
the catch. Shrimpers have to be careful. Clothing
or hands can easily get caught in the machinery.
Broken fingers, **dislocated** shoulders, and strained
backs are part of the job.

The nets are emptied onto the deck. They always
contain more than just shrimp. Fish and crabs get
caught in the nets, too. They must be separated
from the shrimp and returned to the sea. The shrimp
are packed in ice to keep them fresh. The nets are
cleaned and then lowered into the water again.

Ropes, pulleys, and long
poles swing out the nets
as this shrimp trawler
gets ready for work.

No Bones About It

Shrimp — like crabs and lobsters — are **crustaceans.** These are animals that have no bones. They live in shells. The shell acts like a skeleton. It supports and protects the shrimp's soft body. A shrimp's shell is made up of pieces. There are joints where the pieces meet. This lets the shrimp bend and move.

Some shrimp boats from Texas stay out on the Gulf for two weeks or more. They fish at night. That's when the shrimp are moving around, looking for food. Night fishing is more dangerous. Fog may fill the air. Boats risk tangling their nets or running into each other.

Storms are one of the greatest dangers to shrimpers. In shallow water, where most shrimp live, storm waves move faster and are closer together. These waves can easily tip over a shrimp boat or wash the crew overboard.

"Shrimply" delicious! These tasty crustaceans are on the way to markets and restaurants.

Hurricane Katrina

In August 2005, a terrible storm hit the Gulf Coast. Hurricane Katrina blew away fishing boats, docks, and buildings. In Louisiana and Mississippi, almost half of the shrimp boats were destroyed. Many shrimpers could not afford to fix their boats or buy new ones. Many of the ice factories that the shrimpers needed closed down. So did many of the factories that packaged the shrimp.

Gulf Coast shrimpers have faced danger for many years. Those who are left want to keep their trawlers running. Shrimping on the Gulf is what they love to do.

Shrimp, Time, and Tides

Shrimp like warm, shallow water. They have to keep moving to find it because the water in the Gulf keeps changing. Like all oceans, the Gulf of Mexico has tides. The pull of the sun and the moon on Earth causes tides. At high tide, the water near shore is much deeper. At low tide, the water is shallower. The times of the high and low tides change a little bit each day. To find shrimp, boat captains have to pay attention to the tides.

The terrible power of Hurricane Katrina tossed these fishing boats into a pile on the Louisiana shore.

CHAPTER 5

THE WHALERS OF THE CHUKCHI SEA

It is April on the northwestern coast of Alaska. The Chukchi Sea is covered with ice. In a few places, the ice is beginning to break apart. Dark patches of open water called leads can be seen. Along the shore, small groups of men stand silently in the cold, watching the leads. They are Native Alaskans, waiting for bowhead whales. If a whale rises in the open water near them, they will try to kill it.

Keeping Their Culture

Native Alaskans have been hunting whales on the Chukchi Sea for hundreds of years. Long ago, they needed the whale meat to stay alive. They have other food now, but they still want to hunt whales. A writer named Peter Jenkins went whaling with some of these hunters. He said, "Today there is no fear of starvation. They don't want their **culture** to be lost. They want to be like their great-great-great grandfathers."

Native whalers paddle toward a bowhead whale in the Arctic Ocean near Barrow, Alaska.

Many things have changed for Native whalers in recent years. Their homes are made of wood and cement instead of sealskins or ice. They ride to the whaling areas on snowmobiles instead of dogsleds. But the whale hunt is much like it was hundreds of years ago. And it is dangerous work.

Whale Oil

In 1700, a huge sperm whale was caught on a beach in Massachusetts. People cut it up and cooked it. They found that boiling the whale's blubber, or fat, made oil. The oil could be burned in lamps to give light. Soon, ships from many countries were hunting sperm whales. They killed thousands of them, all around the world. The oil we use today — petroleum — was found in the ground in 1859. After that, hunting whales for oil slowed down. Within fifteen years, it had stopped. By then, however, nearly all of the sperm whales were gone. Few are left today.

Waiting on the Ice

The whalers use small, narrow boats. Some are made of wood. Other boats have wooden frames covered with sealskins. Each boat has oars and a spear called a **harpoon.** A long rope and a float are attached to the harpoon. A whaling captain leads each boat.

The whalers carry their boats out onto the ice. Just being on the ice in spring is dangerous. Strong ocean currents carry huge chunks of moving ice that can smash into ice near the shore. The shore ice may break off and float away. In 1997, a piece of ice 30 miles (48 kilometers) long was knocked loose. There were 143 people on the ice, and they drifted in fog and snow

Villagers in Barrow, Alaska, haul a whale out of the ocean after it is killed.

for seven days. At last, they were rescued by U.S. Coast Guard helicopters. Nearly every year, hunters are trapped on broken ice and carried away. Some are never seen again.

Patience and Muscle

The whalers must be very patient. They get as close as they can to an opening in the ice, then wait for a whale to come up. If a whale is spotted, the captain gives a command. The boats are quickly put into the sea. The whalers have only a few seconds to get

Saving Whales, Saving Whaling

By the 1970s, whales were disappearing. Some kinds of whales were **extinct.** Other kinds were **endangered.** In 1977, countries around the world agreed to stop all whale hunting. Native Alaskans didn't like this because whaling was part of their way of life. After a few years, the law was changed. Native Alaskans were allowed to kill a small number of whales each year. In return, the hunters promised to protect the whale's **habitat.**

to the whale and harpoon it. They can't chase a whale in their small boats.

If a whale is killed, the boat crews pull it to the edge of the ice. They send word to their village. Everyone comes to help to pull the whale onto the ice. They use large ropes and lots of muscle. Bowhead whales are huge. They can be 40 feet (12 m) long and weigh 80,000 pounds (36,300 kg).

Once the whale is on shore, it is cut up. One-third is given to the captain and his crew. The rest is divided among the people of the village. Some of the meat is saved for festivals during the year.

Native Alaskan whalers honor the ways of the past. They also follow today's laws about whaling. They want to make sure there will be whales in the Chukchi Sea for their grandchildren to hunt.

Every Day Is an Adventure

Deep-sea fishermen face storms, winds, and high waves. Sharks, whales, and icebergs may be part of their work. They may be injured by nets, hooks, or machinery. Drowning is always a danger.

Fishermen face other problems, too. In some places, like the Grand Banks, there are fewer fish to catch. Frozen fish and other seafood are brought into the United States from other countries. Cheaper foreign fish makes it harder for U.S. fishermen to get a good price for their catch.

Fishing is hard, dangerous work. But few fishermen want to change jobs. One Alaskan salmon fisherman said, "Every day on the boat is an adventure. Who'd want to do anything else?"

People around the world share "the bounty of the sea" — fish, shrimp, clams, and more — thanks to the work of deep-sea fishermen.

29

GLOSSARY

banned — not allowed

bow — the front of a boat or ship

crustaceans — animals that have hard shells but no bones, such as a shrimp or lobsters

culture — the language, beliefs, history, and behaviors of a people

current — water that always moves in the same direction

dislocated — put a bone out of its normal position next to another bone

dories — small rowboats with flat bottoms and high sides

endangered — at risk of becoming extinct

extinct — completely gone; no longer living

gillnetters — fishing boats that use large nets rolled up on drums, or people who work on such boats

habitat — the place in nature where an animal or a plant lives

harpoon — a kind of spear with a rope attached to it, used to kill whales

holds — storage areas in the bottom of ships

hypothermia — a condition that occurs when the temperature of a body goes far below normal

navigation — the science of using a compass, maps, stars, and other tools to find a way from place to place

nutrients — substances that support life and help growth

rapids — very rough, fast-moving water in a river

reproduce — to have babies

sonar — equipment that uses sound waves to find things underwater

stern — the back of a boat or ship

trawlers — boats that drag nets through the water to catch fish

TO FIND OUT MORE

Books

The Cod's Tale. Mark Kurlansky (Putnam Juvenile)

Fishing. America at Work (series). Ann Love and Jane Drake (Kids Can Press)

Salmon Summer. Bruce McMillan (Houghton Mifflin Company)

Seas and Oceans. Nature's Record Breakers (series). Antonella Meucci (Gareth Stevens, Inc.)

Shrimp. Science Under the Sea (series). Lynn Stone (Rourke Publishing, LLC)

Web Sites

American Cetacean Society: Bowhead Whale
www.acsonline.org/factpack/bowhead.htm
Find out more about the whale that Native Alaskans hunt as part of their culture.

Life Stage of a Salmon
www.cf.adfg.state.ak.us/geninfo/research/genetics/kids/salstory.php
Learn more about how salmon develop, swim, and spawn.

Enchanted Learning: Shrimp
www.enchantedlearning.com/subjects/invertebrates/crustacean/Shrimp.shtml
See diagrams of shrimp, and learn about their life cycle.

A Whale Watch Report
www.sciencenewsforkids.org/articles/20050323/Feature1.asp
Learn about whale hunting and modern-day dangers to whales.

INDEX

About the Author

William David Thomas lives in Rochester, New York, where he works with special-needs students. Bill has written software documentation, magazine articles, training programs, annual reports, books for children, a few poems, and lots of letters. He likes to go backpacking and canoeing, play his guitar, and obsess about baseball. Bill claims he was once King of Fiji but gave up the throne to pursue a career as a relief pitcher. It's not true.